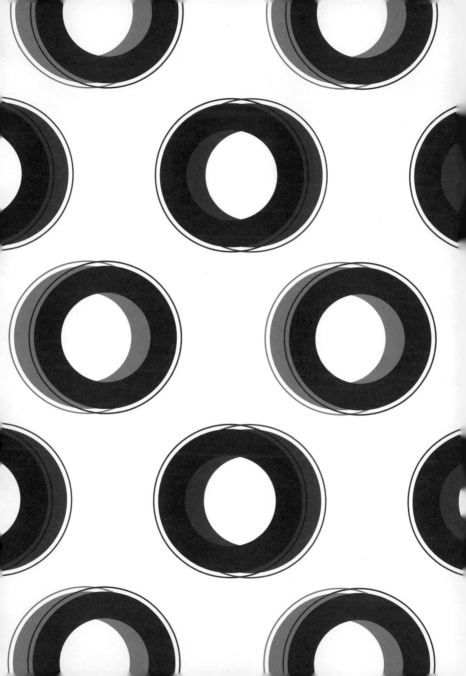

a **short guide** to a

Happy Divorce

13-Digit ISBN: 978-1-64643-062-8
10-Digit ISBN: 1-64643-062-X

This book may be ordered by mail from the publisher. Please include $5.99 for postage and handling. Please support your local bookseller first!

Books published by Cider Mill Press Book Publishers are available at special discounts for bulk purchases in the United States by corporations, institutions, and other organizations. For more information, please contact the publisher.

Cider Mill Press Book Publishers
"Where good books are ready for press"
PO Box 454
12 Spring Street
Kennebunkport, Maine 04046

Visit us online!
cidermillpress.com

Typography: Proxima Nova, Begum

Printed in China
1 2 3 4 5 6 7 8 9 0
First Edition

a **short guide** to a

Happy
Divorce

Sharon Gilchrest O'Neill, Ed.S.

CIDER MILL PRESS

BOOK
PUBLISHERS
KENNEBUNKPORT, MAINE

A happy divorce?

That truly sounds like an oxymoron, and it is for many divorced couples and families. But then, when have you heard a couple's goal to be a happy divorce? You may think it absurd! To move toward a happy divorce may feel like you are acquiescing and no longer fighting for what is right. But what *is* right?

Most couples can end up with a marriage far better than the one they started with.

My experience working with divorcing couples has shown me so much of what is wrong: spouses and their children screaming, literally and figuratively in pain, needy, and seeking help in all the wrong places. Divorce comes to define them. Divorce creates victims with lots of complicated baggage. None of this bodes well for the "happily ever after" that everyone deserves.

But let me digress for a moment to say a few things about marriage and about bringing it to an end. For the record, saving marriages has been my lifelong passion. I believe that most marriages are repairable and worth every bit of the terribly difficult work required. My enduring hopefulness stems from knowing that once a couple has made their relationship *the* priority, and taken the pieces apart and put things back together differently, most couples can end up with a marriage far better than the one they started with.

I expect spouses to fight hard for their marriage and their family, and to use every resource at their disposal to find inspiration and then solutions to their unique and complex problems. Often, even one spouse, alone for a time in therapy, can make important inroads to helping the marriage. But in the end it always takes two to complete the work. My clients have taught me that: marrying quickly after a whirlwind courtship, being complete opposites, never fighting, and having competing careers or contentious values, do not hold a marriage together over the years. Sometimes there is just not enough of the right stuff, or it really is much-too-little, much-too-late and a marriage cannot, and should not, be saved.

But in the end it always takes two to complete the work.

Sometimes there is just not enough of the right stuff.

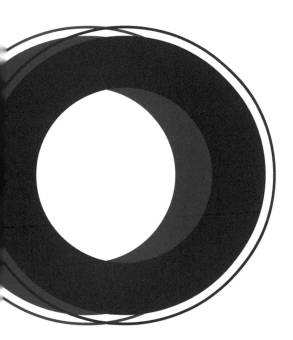

When all has been tried, and every path exhausted, including working with a professional who concedes that the marriage cannot be saved, only then does divorce become the inevitable solution.

When a marriage has become destructive,

or a partner is apathetic and unwilling to work on change, it is time to let go of the possibility of restoring the relationship. It is not the time to have "last hope sex" with your spouse. It is not the time for a rebound fling. These kinds of behaviors will only leave you shaky and disoriented for the divorce effort ahead.

A new reality will begin to take hold. The feelings of loss in a divorce become much less about the loss of a spouse, but rather about the loss of the life you've created over the years. Take honest stock of your partner: Have you been enjoying spending time together? Did you want to have children together? Had you been looking forward to your "empty nesting" life after your children were launched, or when you retired? Have you continued to help each other to be the best you can be?

In my work with divorcing couples they eventually come to recognize and acknowledge similar truths about the problems in their relationship.

Have you continued to help each other to be the best you can be?

This decision will be one of the most significant in your life; it is huge.

Why did the marriage become unhealthy? Why did the marriage no longer meet their needs? I believe that partners do owe each other help in understanding as best as possible how and why divorce became the only solution. It allows one to place guilt and remorse in proper perspective. It helps in accepting one's responsibility – even if only for a lack of insight or judgment in marrying a partner who was not a good fit, or in not having understood more about oneself.

I urge couples to do this work. Increased insight lowers the risk of finding yourself repeating the same choices and behaviors in your future relationships. Second marriages have a higher incidence of divorce for this reason.

When divorce becomes the final answer, spouses often realize they have not been loved as they wanted and deserved to be, and now they have another chance for happiness and fulfillment. Often the partner who was not the initiator comes to see that their spouse has actually done them a favor. Both come to agree that the marriage was fundamentally unhappy.

This decision will be one of the most significant in your life; it is huge. There is no downplaying it. As much as you may not believe in divorce, or want to be divorced, you need to make peace with the fact that the decision is not yours alone, and that you have done all that is humanly possible. Now it is time to shift gears and revise perspectives: divorce *is* the right path and the healthy path for you and your spouse. There is no longer happiness in your marriage. The goal is to find happiness in divorcing.

How do you begin?

Slowly. Very slowly.

When we are no longer able to change a situation, we are challenged to change ourselves.

—Viktor E. Frankl

Do not run out and share your saga with the world!

Divorce can feel like your world has utterly collapsed. Or even that it has disappeared. It is surreal. It is necessary to take time and space to be alone. To think. Do not run out and share your saga with the world!

Do not run out and share your saga with the world!

I have never had a client who wished they had told more people sooner. Those who did regretted it deeply. Rely on a few trusted friends and family members until you have gained further clarity on your divorce and better understand how you will tell your story. The story of the end of your marriage will be part of the legacy of your life and the future of you and your family. Stay cautious and protective. Take care to rein in the desire to expose or punish your spouse. Better that most people hear the short story — the abridged edition.

Divorce is a profound loss in anyone's life. Even if you are the initiator. Even if it is amicable. You will feel a range of emotions: shock, fear, anger, sadness, acceptance, and relief. The feelings will come and go in waves that allow you to grieve. It is natural and normal. It is healthy.

What is not healthy is allowing divorce to just happen to you.

It is unfortunate that unlike the effort we put into beginnings — engagements, wedding vows, getting married — too many couples forge ahead into divorce haphazardly without goals and a plan. They just want it over. They just want to move on. But we owe it to our families and ourselves to take even greater care with the ending of a marriage. How you handle yourself during this major life change will

The feelings will come and go in waves that allow you to grieve.

impact everyone you love, everyone who cares about you. It will take delicacy and the utmost sensitivity to do no harm.

Divorce will become the most transformative undertaking of your life.

Finding your way through will require great attention and focus. You will need to use all the best of your skills to communicate, organize, follow-up, and follow-through. The bigger picture and the long view will be your most trustworthy guidance system. What do you want to happen? How do you want it to happen? Determine and never lose sight of the healthy outcomes you envision. Commit them to writing and keep them close to your heart. For example: I want to enjoy life with a new companion or partner one day, without the angry baggage so characteristic of those who have experienced divorce; I want my

Divorce will become the most transformative undertaking of your life.

I want my children to thrive in all the ways in which they are capable, despite this divorce.

children to thrive in all the ways in which they are capable, despite this divorce.

If there are children,

they will be your priority and *the* motivation for doing your divorce responsibly — with decency and honesty. They deserve it. There are two truths that are best to accept very early on: first, children desperately need both parents; and second, they desperately need both parents communicating together on their behalf. No child should be placed in the middle of an ugly or hostile situation. My experience has shown me, without doubt that children ultimately and over time watch and feel all the truth. Actions based on revenge will only emerge later as heavy burdens to bear. Find strength in your dignity.

Stay as non-adversarial as possible with your spouse. Listen calmly and completely. What is logical and loving? What is equitable and decent? What is truly best? You and your spouse may no longer be able to provide a happy marriage and secure home *together*, but you *can* provide two loving parents who share the priority of continuing to care for and protect your children. I encourage parents to view themselves as business partners now, allied in the cause of their lives. Vow that failure is unacceptable.

And if there was ever a moment in your parenting effort to think "quality time" with your children, this is it. Turn off the technology and

Find strength in your dignity.

just *be* with your child. Initiate new rituals that can be cathartic over these months. Remind your children often that you are there for them, no matter what. They need to know they can count on you more than ever during a divorce. *Always* keep your word. And even when the going gets tough, don't fall into the Disneyland syndrome. Don't succumb to the temptation of buying love.

None of this will be easy. It will demand all the patience and selflessness you can muster. *Vow* to take the high road; it will be fulfilling and immeasurably worth it in the end. Some parents become superb role models, even heroes. Best that you both do!

Remind your children often that you are there for them, no matter what.

Whether there are children or not,

Vow that you will not go to war. War never goes well, nor ends well. And no one ever, ever wins.

Do everything that you can to stay out of the court system. Mediate. Negotiate. Give and take. Give a little more. Brainstorm together for resourceful and reasonable resolutions. *Vow* to not let attorneys think or speak for you. Do you really want the dog or are you just trying to hurt your spouse? Do not give up on each other. Persevere. Have faith that you can do this together!

Many ask: Is it truly possible to have an amicable divorce with a respectful ending? I do believe it is possible *if* spouses agree and commit to such a goal. It will not happen by accident and you will both need to believe that civility can be maintained throughout the divorce process.

Two important concepts to guide you:

The first: **Good-Faith Negotiation**

Have faith that you can do this together!

Commit to each other to negotiate with good faith.

Going forward amicably requires, first and foremost, honoring what is called "good-faith negotiation" efforts. That implies that each spouse is not just looking out for themselves, but will behave with honesty and integrity throughout the process. Such negotiation is essential in resolving the critical necessity for full financial disclosure.

Both of you will need to have *all* financial information and documents. Copies of everything! If one spouse has been in the dark about finances, which is often the case with couples, that spouse will now need to be completely involved. No one can stay in the dark. Transparency is required. It will build trust as division of assets, alimony, custody, and child support are determined. Ultimately unique financial plans are needed for both of you to transition into your new lives. Commit to each other to negotiate with good faith.

The second: **Divorcing Without Blame**

Once the divorce decision has been made and you are taking the first steps toward a plan, it is crucial to stop questioning the past. Rehashing and fixating on resentments and wounds will only escalate into bad behaviors, risking your most important future goals. In my experience with clients, I have found it essential that spouses understand that the court system will never give them emotional justice. Do not let your anger and pain derail your psychological and physical health, or your economic well-being.

It is crucial to stop questioning the past.

You and your spouse

have done the work of assessing the relationship and have agreed that the marriage is broken. It cannot be fixed. Ultimately, it doesn't matter who initiated this new life. Do keep in mind, however, if you are the initiator, your spouse will need time and empathy to catch up emotionally. This is not a time to be anything less than understanding and generous. It will be most productive to be able to talk through the divorce plan without the need to keep blaming each other. Make the effort to catch yourself when blaming and shut it down. This will not be easy. But you will have a much better chance of working through an amicable settlement that will give you your very best outcome, and one that will be fair. Both parties must commit to divorcing without blame.

Keep reminding yourself to focus on the big picture to guide you through the divorce process. It is not about myriad details. Imagine life beyond divorce for *everyone* involved. Take the necessary time to understand what is truly important for you. Write it down. Go over it such that you will be able to express with clarity

Imagine life beyond divorce for everyone involved.

It is hard work to end a marriage well.

your desires in a calm manner. Think through what you believe your spouse will want, to help prepare yourself. Imagine both sides of the future living arrangements. Do you really want to keep your current home? Do you honestly want full child custody?

Most divorced couples still need to be connected in some way with their ex-spouse. What kind of relationship do you envision? Consider what you can simply let go of. Whether your marriage has been many decades long or just years, with or without children, your future life is at stake. Trying to punish your spouse, or fighting over parenting issues almost guarantees a divorce that will not be amicable.

It is hard work to end a marriage well. It takes concentration. It takes effort. Give this work your full attention; you cannot disengage. Your divorce has been in the making for a long time, the ending of it will take time too. Don't be rushed. There will be very difficult decisions to be made. You will need to compromise and negotiate. There will be differences of opinions and arguments. You will give in. Your spouse will give in. You will need to find patience over and over again. You will not be entirely happy. You will not get everything you want. The more you can talk together and negotiate your own settlement, there can be a marriage ending for both spouses that hasn't resulted in financial ruin or emotional devastation.

Continue with your therapist during the divorce process. It will help you both to stay on track and in control of your coping skills. It will be a safe place to discuss the difficult decisions, particularly when emotions are at a high point. A divorce attorney does not have the formal

You will need to find patience over and over again.

It will be more likely that you can divorce with some level of mediation and save time, money, and good will.

training to help with this. There is irony in that a good divorce process demands skills that are also helpful in marriage. Some further guidance with a professional can greatly help throughout the process.

It will be more likely that you can divorce with some level of mediation and save time, money, and good will.

Divorcing is but one stage of your life,

and it *will* come to an end. The more you can do to have an amicable divorce will leave you better prepared, with energy and motivation to build a new life.

Believe in your ability to choose how you respond to this loss. You do not want to make choices that you will regret and have to live with forever. Get it as right as you can. There really are no second chances when it comes to divorce.

Know there will be times when you feel unmoored, when it all gets to be too much. Take a break, and if only for a few moments, walk outside and sit on a bench in the sun and take ten deep breaths, or call a best friend. Be careful to keep yourself physically healthy and strong. Eat right, stay rested, don't self-medicate, and keep medical appointments. This is not a time to let yourself go.

It is, though, a time to learn. A positive aspect of loss is that it creates the opportunity for change. Challenge assumptions about the life you have

A positive aspect of loss is that it creates the opportunity for change.

You may come to realize valuable parts of yourself have been lost along the way.

been living; many find they have not been living their best life at all. Define what will make you happy or unhappy. Gain new perspectives about what is vital in the evolving context of your new life. You may come to realize valuable parts of yourself have been lost along the way. Why not rescue some of those old goals and dreams?

Talk about these questions with a close friend, family member, or therapist. They can help remind you of things you have abandoned about yourself. Reminiscing can bring you back to desires you had let go. Consider anew what you truly value in life.

Many making their way through divorce are pleasantly surprised with their newfound capabilities: managing their own 401(k) investments; making the holiday or vacation travel plans; being the one to comfort the children when they awake from a frightening dream and then easing them back to sleep.

Vow to not let divorce ruin the rest of your life.

No matter the reason, divorce is a heartbreaking ending to a marriage, but not the end of a life. It can instead be the beginning of things new and wonderful that you have never imagined. You will start to find moments of new meaning. And one day you will actually wake up refreshed for the first time in a long time, eagerly looking forward to your new life. There will be steadfast family and friends. There will be passion and love again with a new partner or companion, a change in career or a new home.

Keep your divorce vows. The ones you've read about here and other personal ones that you and your partner agree to in planning your divorce. Write them up and keep copies that you

Vow to not let divorce ruin the rest of your life.

reread often. You can make them happen. You will both be proud. You will gain the strength to rebuild your life. You will be secure in knowing you have done all you could. There will be few regrets.

Significant losses in life – whether a death, a job, one's health or marriage – change us forever. Stay open to all that you learn and know that you will continue to learn long afterward. Loss will reward you if you can define and accept its gifts.

Our lives don't always turn out the way we envisioned. Our dreams don't always come true.

During their darkest days my clients have surprised me with the strength and courage to make the most difficult decisions and thereby create new lives. Their hurt fades. They take comfort in the good memories and find it in their hearts to be able to continue to care about their

ex-spouse's well-being. Some even become friends again.

For yourself and for your spouse make a happy divorce your goal. Be guided by the bigger picture and the long view.

Do no harm.

Vow to stay on the high road.

I wish you the "happily ever after" that you deserve!

To find a well-trained and compassionate
therapist to work with go to:
Therapist Locator

Service of AAMFT (American Association for
Marriage and Family Therapists)

Sharon Gilchrest O'Neill, Ed.S.

is a licensed marriage and family therapist
and the author of *A Short Guide to a
Happy Marriage*, and its *Gay Edition*, *Sheltering
Thoughts About Loss and Grief*, and *Lur'ning:
147 Inspiring Thoughts for Learning on the Job*.
She has worked both in private practice and
the corporate setting, helping her clients to
examine assumptions, think creatively, and build
upon strengths. O'Neill holds three degrees in
psychology and is often called on as an expert
by a variety of publications, including the *Wall
Street Journal*, the *New York Times*, the *Boston
Globe*, and *HuffPost*.

About Cider Mill Press
Book Publishers

Good ideas ripen with time. From seed to harvest, Cider Mill Press brings fine reading, information, and entertainment together between the covers of its creatively crafted books. Our Cider Mill bears fruit twice a year, publishing a new crop of titles each spring and fall.

"Where Good Books Are Ready for Press"

Visit us online at
cidermillpress.com
or write to us at
PO Box 454
12 Spring St.
Kennebunkport, Maine 04046

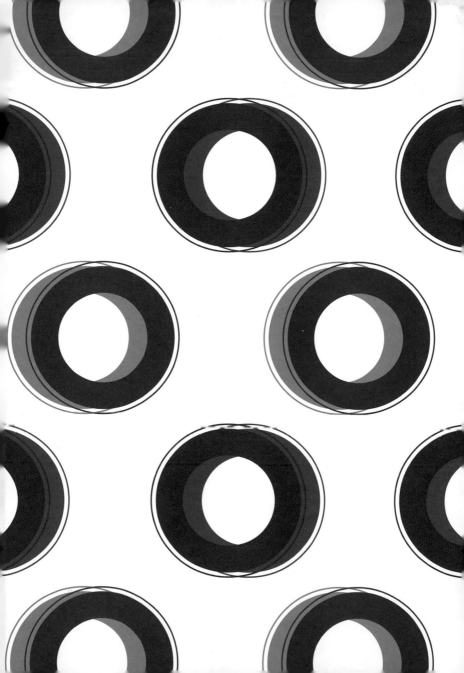

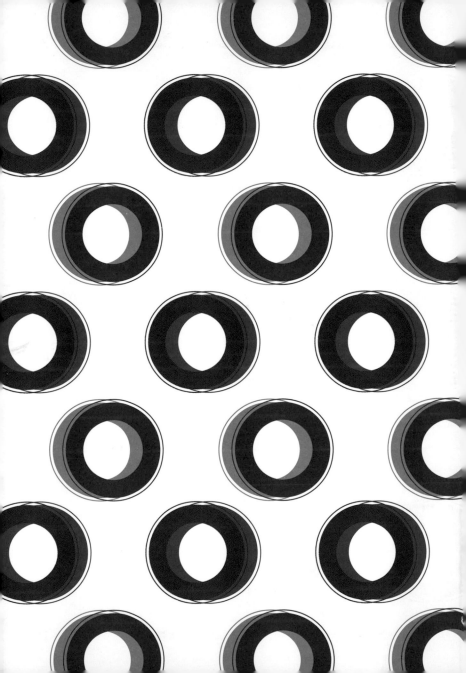